"Are the thoughts I am thinking going to lead me to my desired goal?"

-Alia Yasmin Khan

TABLE OF CONTENTS

CHAPTER 1 **The Power of Conscious Creation** 7

CHAPTER 2 **The Journey of Mind** 11

CHAPTER 3 **Mental Duality** 17

CHAPTER 4 **The Seven Mental Faculties** 23

CHAPTER 5 **Observation** 29

CHAPTER 6 **Writing** 35

CHAPTER 7 **Listening** 41

CHAPTER 8 **Speech** 47

CHAPTER 9 **The Integration** 53

CHAPTER 10 **Mastering Resistance** 59

CHAPTER 11 **The Field Effect** 65

CHAPTER 12 **Quantum Resilience** 71

CHAPTER 13 **The Language of Creation** 77

CHAPTER 14 **The Momentum Principle** 83

CHAPTER 15 **Quantum Leaps** 89

CHAPTER 16 **Identity Shift** 95

CHAPTER 17 **Field Mastery** 101

CHAPTER 18 **The Awakening** 107

CHAPTER 1

**The Power of Conscious Creation:
Your Mind's Ultimate Reality Engine**

On a crisp winter morning in Phoenix, I sat across from Sarah, a successful tech executive who seemed to have everything - except peace. "I'm doing all the right things," she confided, "but it feels like I'm fighting reality itself."

Her words echoed a truth I'd discovered through years of research and transformation work: Most people aren't living - they're reacting to a reality they don't realize they're creating.

Recent research from the HeartMath Institute reveals something extraordinary about human consciousness. Your thoughts and emotions generate an electromagnetic field that extends up to six feet beyond your body, literally shaping the physical world around you.

Dr. Joe Dispenza's groundbreaking studies show that when you change your mental patterns, you change not just your brain's neural architecture but the very fabric of reality you experience.

Consider this: Right now, your brain is processing 400 billion bits of information per second, yet you're consciously aware of only 2,000 bits.

What determines which bits reach your awareness? Your conscious and unconscious programming. This isn't philosophy - it's neurobiology.

Take a moment now. Close your eyes and bring your awareness to your breath. As you inhale, imagine drawing in pure potential. As you exhale, release old patterns of limitation. This simple practice begins rewiring your neural pathways for conscious creation.

Let's return to Sarah's story. Through implementing the principles you'll learn in this book, she discovered something remarkable. Her reality wasn't happening to her - it was happening through her.

Within six months of applying conscious creation principles:
- Her stress levels dropped by 70%
- Her income increased by 40%
- Her relationships transformed
- Her sense of purpose clarified

Brain scans taken before and after implementing these practices show remarkable changes. The prefrontal cortex - your brain's conscious creation center - shows increased activity and neural density. The amygdala - your fear center - shows reduced reactivity.

Take out your transformation journal (you'll want to keep one throughout this journey). Write down three areas of your life where you feel like reality is happening to you rather than through you. These are your initial focus points for conscious creation.

Here is a two-minute consciousness alignment:
1. Sit comfortably
2. Focus on your breath
3. Visualize your desired reality
4. Feel it as already present

Before moving to Chapter 2, reflect:
- What patterns in your life feel beyond your control?
- Where do you sense untapped potential?
- What does your ideal reality look like and how does this life experience feel to you?

In the next chapter, we'll explore the science of mind and how your thoughts literally reshape your brain's neural architecture.

Remember: You're not just reading a book - you're activating your conscious creator.

CHAPTER 2

The Journey of Mind:

Understanding Your Reality Creation Engine

The soft morning light filtered through the office window as Michael, a successful surgeon, sat across from me, his expression a mixture of frustration and curiosity. "I understand the brain," he said, "but I don't understand my mind."

His statement perfectly captures the journey we're about to embark upon - understanding the profound difference between your brain's mechanical operations and your mind's reality-creating power.

Your mind isn't just a product of your brain - it's the conductor of a magnificent neural orchestra. Recent research from the Max Planck Institute for Brain Research reveals something extraordinary:

Your thoughts don't just reflect your reality; they precede and create it.

When you think a thought, you're not just having an idea - you're initiating a cascade of neural events that literally reshape your brain's physical structure.

Consider this: Every thought you think creates a neural pathway. Think the same thought repeatedly, and you strengthen that pathway until it becomes your default pattern of reality creation.

Research shows that these neural pathways become so efficient that they operate below conscious awareness, creating your reality. The subconscious programs which are prewired are constantly creating our experiences.

Let's explore what this means through Thomas's story. As a business owner, Thomas couldn't understand why his company kept hitting the same revenue ceiling despite different strategies.

During our work together, we discovered his neural pathways were literally programmed for limitation. Every time he thought about growth, his brain activated neural networks associated with struggle and scarcity.

Through conscious reprogramming, Thomas began creating new neural pathways:
Instead of thinking "growth is hard," he practiced thinking "growth is easy".

Rather than focusing on limitations, he directed his attention to possibilities.

Where he once saw obstacles, he trained his mind to see opportunities

The transformation was remarkable. Within six months:
- His revenue doubled
- Team performance improved dramatically
- Innovation became natural
- Stress levels dropped significantly

But here's what makes this understanding powerful: You're doing this programming every moment, whether you realize it or not. Every thought, every emotion, every focus of attention is either strengthening pathways of success or reinforcing patterns of limitation.

Take a moment now. Close your eyes and bring your awareness to your thoughts. Notice how each thought creates a subtle feeling in your body. This awareness is the first step in conscious neural programming.

Recent studies using functional MRI scans show that consistent thought patterns literally change your brain's physical structure. Areas associated with your dominant thoughts show increased neural density and activity.

In your transformation journal, write down:
- Three thought patterns that dominate your daily experience
- The reality each thought pattern is creating
- The new thought pattern you choose to cultivate

Let's conclude with a neural reprogramming meditation:
1. Sit comfortably and close your eyes
2. Observe your current thought patterns without judgment
3. Visualize new neural pathways forming
4. Feel the reality these new pathways create

Remember: Your mind isn't just experiencing reality - it's creating it through precise neural programming.

In your transformation journal, write down:
 - Three thought patterns that dominate your daily experience
 - The reality each thought pattern is creating
 - The new thought pattern you choose to cultivate

Let's conclude with a neural reprogramming meditation:
1. Sit comfortably and close your eyes
2. Observe your current thought patterns without judgment
3. Visualize new neural pathways forming
4. Feel the reality these new pathways create

Remember: Your mind isn't just experiencing reality - it's creating it through precise neural programming.

CHAPTER 3

Mental Duality:

Power of Conscious Choice

The late afternoon sun cast long shadows across the office as Jessica, a talented entrepreneur, shared her frustration. "I keep visualizing success," she said, "but my mind constantly drifts to what could go wrong."

Her experience perfectly illustrates the principle of Mental Duality - the mind's tendency to focus either on what we want or what we fear.

Let me share something that transformed my understanding of how reality works. While exploring and researching the HeartMath Institute, we discovered that your brain processes positive and negative thoughts through entirely different neural networks.

When you focus on what you want, you activate the prefrontal cortex - your brain's creation center. When you focus on what you fear, you activate the amygdala - your survival center. You can't fully activate both simultaneously.

Think about this: Every moment of your conscious experience, you're making a choice - often unconsciously - between creation and survival thinking. Dr. Lisa Feldman Barrett's groundbreaking research shows that your brain doesn't just process reality - it predicts it based on your dominant thought patterns.

When you consistently focus on what you want, your brain literally rewires itself to spot opportunities that support that reality.

Consider Maria's transformation. As a real estate investor, she struggled with consistent success until she understood Mental Duality. She noticed her mind habitually focused on:

- Potential market crashes instead of growth opportunities
- Difficult clients instead of ideal partnerships
- Financial risks instead of wealth creation
- Problems to solve instead of successes to celebrate

Through conscious application of Mental Duality principles, she began directing her focus toward:
- Market opportunities and growth trends
- Ideal client experiences and partnerships
- Wealth creation and financial abundance
- Solutions and successes

The transformation was remarkable. Within four months:
- Her property portfolio doubled
- Client relationships improved dramatically
- Income increased by 60%
- Stress levels decreased significantly

Take a moment now. Close your eyes and bring awareness to your current thought patterns. Notice where your mind naturally drifts - toward what you want or what you fear? This awareness is the first step in mastering Mental Duality.

Recent neuroimaging studies show that consistent focus on desired outcomes literally strengthens neural pathways associated with success while weakening fear-based circuits. This isn't motivation - it's neural reprogramming.

Let's practice Mental Duality meditation:
1. Sit comfortably and close your eyes
2. Notice any fear-based thoughts without judgment
3. Consciously shift focus to your desired reality
4. Feel the emotional state of having what you want

Remember: Your mind is always focusing somewhere. The question isn't whether you're creating through focus - you're doing that every moment.

The question is: Are you focusing by design or by default?

In Chapter 4, we'll explore how to use the Seven Mental Faculties to accelerate your reality creation. You're not just reading about transformation - you're rewiring your brain for success.

Before moving forward, consider:
- Where does your mind naturally focus?
- What reality is this focus creating?
- What focus would serve your highest good?

Your transformation isn't about fighting negative thoughts - it's about consciously choosing where to direct your mental energy. Every moment presents this choice.

Choose wisely.

CHAPTER 4

The Seven Mental Faculties:

Your Mind's Control Center

As I sit my morning coffee sitting across from me was David, a brilliant tech entrepreneur, shared his frustration. "I understand software programming," he said, "but I can't seem to program my own mind for success."

His words perfectly captured why understanding your seven mental faculties is crucial for conscious reality creation.

Think of your mental faculties as the control panel of your consciousness. Just as a pilot must master multiple instruments to fly effectively, you must understand and harmonize your mental faculties to create your desired reality.

Recent research from the Department of Cognitive Neuroscience at Stanford reveals something extraordinary: These seven faculties - Perception, Reason, Will, Memory, Imagination, Intuition, and Emotion - operate through distinct neural networks that can be consciously strengthened and directed.

Let me share Amanda's story, which perfectly illustrates the power of mastering these faculties. As a successful attorney, she excelled at using reason but struggled with intuition and imagination.

Her reality reflected this imbalance - logical success but creative limitation. Through conscious faculty development, she transformed her experience entirely.

Let's explore each faculty through the lens of modern neuroscience:
Perception isn't just about seeing - it's your reality filter. Dr. Karl Friston's research shows that your brain creates what he calls a "predictive model" of reality based on your perceptual patterns.

When Amanda shifted her perception from "life is a struggle" to "life is an opportunity," her brain literally began filtering reality differently.

Reason serves as your internal logic center.
But here's what most people miss: Logic should serve your dreams, not limit them. Neuroscience shows that balanced reasoning actually enhances creativity rather than restricting it.

Will isn't about force - it's about focused attention. Dr. Andrew Huberman's research reveals that willpower operates through the prefrontal cortex's ability to maintain focused attention on desired outcomes.

Memory isn't just about storing information - it's your tool for future creation. Every memory you hold shapes your expectation and therefore, your reality. Recent studies show that consciously reframing memories literally rewires your brain's predictive patterns.
Imagination activates the same neural networks as actual experience. When you vividly imagine success, you're literally programming your brain for that reality. The research

shows that imagined experiences create measurable changes in your body's electromagnetic field.

Intuition processes billions of bits of information per second through your subconscious mind. It's not mystical - it's your brain's pattern recognition system operating at quantum speed.

Emotion serves as your reality catalyst. Dr. Candace Pert's research proves that emotions create neuropeptides - molecular messengers that influence every cell in your body.

Take a moment now. Close your eyes and bring awareness to each faculty:
 - Notice what you're perceiving
 - Observe your reasoning patterns
 - Feel your willpower's focus
 - Access an empowering memory
 - Engage your imagination
 - Listen to your intuition
 - Notice your emotional state

In your transformation journal, assess each faculty:
 - Which are your strongest?
 - Which need development?
 - How does each influence your reality?

Practice faculty integration meditation:
1. Sit quietly, eyes closed
2. Consciously engage each faculty
3. Feel them working in harmony
4. Visualize your desired reality

Your mental faculties are always operating.

The question isn't whether they're creating your reality - they are.

The question is: Are you directing them consciously or letting them operate by default?

In Chapter 5, we'll explore how to use these faculties within the OWLS system for maximum transformation. You're not just reading about your mental faculties - you're learning to master them for conscious reality creation.

CHAPTER 5

Observation:

The Art of Conscious Awareness

Before you dismiss observation as simple watching, consider this: Your brain processes 11 million bits of information per second, but your conscious mind only handles about 50 bits.

What determines which 50 bits shape your reality? Your observation patterns.

Dr. Andrew Huberman's research at Stanford reveals something extraordinary about observation: The neural pathways activated by what you consistently observe literally reshape your brain's architecture.

You're not just seeing reality - you're selecting which reality becomes your experience.

Let me share Rachel's story. As a successful marketing executive, she couldn't understand why her life felt stuck despite her achievements. During our first session, I noticed something fascinating about her observation patterns. She consistently observed:
 - Problems to solve rather than opportunities to seize
 - Competitors' successes rather than her own achievements
 - What could go wrong rather than what could go rig
 - Limitations rather than responsibilities

Her observation patterns were literally programming her brain for stress and limitation. But here's what changed everything: Understanding that observation isn't passive - it's creative.

Through conscious application of observation principles, Rachel began directing her awareness toward:
- Opportunities emerging in her field
- Her unique strengths and achievements
- Positive possibilities in every situation
- Resources available for growth

The transformation was remarkable. Within three months:
- Her income increased by 40%
- Innovation became natural
- Relationships improved dramatically
- Stress levels dropped significantly

Take a moment now. Close your eyes and bring awareness to what you're currently observing in your life. Notice the patterns. Are you observing what you want to create or what you want to avoid?

Recent studies using eye-tracking technology show that successful people literally see different aspects of the same situation compared to those who struggle. This isn't motivation - it's neural programming through conscious observation

In your transformation journal, create an observation audit:
- What do you consistently notice about money?

- What patterns do you observe in relationships?
- What do you observe about your capabilities?
- What do you notice about opportunities?

Practice conscious observation meditation:
1. Sit quietly, eyes open
2. Notice what naturally draws your attention
3. Consciously shift focus to what you want to create
4. Feel the difference in your emotional state

Remember: Your observation patterns are either strengthening your success programming or reinforcing your limitations.

The choice isn't whether you're observing - you're doing that every moment.

The choice is what you choose to observe.

In Chapter 6, we'll explore how Writing transforms your subconscious programming. You're not just reading about observation - you're learning to consciously create through what you choose to notice.

CHAPTER 6

Writing:

Programming Your Subconscious Mind

I silenced my phone and I prepared myself and I began to review James's journal. As a successful engineer, he'd documented his journey meticulously, yet something was missing. "I write everything down," he said, "but I'm not seeing the transformation I want."

His experience perfectly illustrates why understanding the neuroscience of writing is crucial for conscious reality creation.

Dr. James Pennebaker's groundbreaking research at the University of Texas reveals something extraordinary: Handwriting activates neural pathways that typing cannot reach.

When you write by hand, you engage both hemispheres of your brain simultaneously, creating what neuroscientists call a "whole-brain state" - optimal for reprogramming your subconscious mind.

Consider this: Every time you write, you're not just recording thoughts - you're creating instructions for your subconscious mind.

Recent studies using functional MRI scans show that handwriting engages 40% more neural regions than typing, creating what researchers call a "neural bridge" between intention and reality.

Let me share Catherine's transformation story. As a corporate executive, she kept detailed digital notes but struggled with consistent success. During our work together, we discovered her writing was unconsciously programming limitation:

Her daily entries focused on:
- Problems to solve
- Deadlines to meet
- Conflicts to manage
- Resources lacking

Through conscious writing practices, she began programming success:
- Opportunities emerging
- Goals manifesting
- Relationships flourishing
- Resources abundant

The transformation was remarkable. Within four months:
- Her leadership impact doubled
- Team performance soared
- Innovation became natural
- Stress levels dropped significantly

Take out your transformation journal now. Using your non-dominant hand, write the word "SUCCESS." Notice how this engages different neural pathways. This awareness is the first step in conscious writing programming.

Recent neuroimaging studies show that conscious writing practices literally reshape your brain's neural architecture. Areas associated with your written focus show increased activity and neural density.

Create your success script:
 1. Write your desired reality in present tense
 2. Include sensory details
 3. Engage emotions
 4. Be specific about outcomes

Practice writing meditation:
 1. Sit with your journal open
 2. Close your eyes and breathe deeply
 3. Connect with your desired reality
 4. Write from that state of consciousness

Remember: Your writing is either programming success or reinforcing limitations.

The choice isn't whether you're programming - you're doing that every time you write.

The choice is what you choose to program.

In Chapter 7, we'll explore how Listening transforms your neural pathways. You're not just learning about writing - you're mastering the art of conscious reality programming through the written word.

Before moving forward, consider:
 - What are you currently programming through your writing?
 - How can you use writing to create your desired reality?
 - What success script will you write today?

CHAPTER 7

Listening:

Programming Your Neural Pathways Through Sound

The morning silence in the office was broken by Sarah's frustrated sigh. "I listen to motivational content all day," she said, "but I'm not seeing the transformation I want." Her experience perfectly captures why understanding the neuroscience of listening is crucial for conscious reality creation.

Dr. Nina Kraus's groundbreaking research at Northwestern University reveals something extraordinary: Sound physically reshapes your brain's neural architecture. When you consciously choose what to listen to, you're not just consuming content - you're literally rewiring your brain's success circuitry.

Consider this: Every sound you hear creates electrical patterns in your brain that either strengthen your success programming or reinforce limitation patterns. Recent studies using advanced EEG mapping show that your brain processes different types of audio input through distinct neural networks, creating what researchers call "sonic blueprints" for reality creation.

Let me share Marcus's transformation story. As a successful real estate investor, he struggled with consistent growth until he understood the power of conscious listening.

His default audio environment included:
 - News about market crashes
 - Conversations about economic uncertainty

- Negative self-talk about limitations
- Worry-filled discussions with colleagues

Through conscious listening practices, he transformed his audio environment to include:
- Success case studies and market opportunities
- Strategic growth conversations
- Empowering self-talk
- Solution-focused team discussions

The transformation was remarkable. Within three months:
- His portfolio value doubled
- Team performance improved dramatically
- Innovation became natural
- Stress levels dropped significantly

Take a moment now. Close your eyes and bring awareness to your current sonic environment. What messages are programming your neural pathways? This awareness is the first step in conscious audio programming.

Recent neuroimaging studies show that consistent exposure to specific types of audio content literally reshapes your brain's neural architecture. Areas associated with your dominant audio input show increased activity and neural density.

Create your success soundscape:
1. Audit your current audio environment
2. Identify success-programming content
3. Create strategic listening schedules
4. Monitor emotional responses to different inputs

Practice sonic awareness meditation:
1. Sit quietly with eyes closed
2. Notice all sounds in your environment
3. Observe their emotional impact
4. Choose sounds that support your success

Remember: Your audio environment is either programming success or reinforcing limitations.

The choice isn't whether you're being programmed - you're receiving audio programming every moment.

The choice is what programming you consciously select.

In Chapter 8, we'll explore how Speech completes the OWLS system by activating your quantum creation field. You're not just learning about listening - you're mastering the art of conscious reality programming through sound.

Before moving forward, consider:
 - What is your current audio environment programming?
 - How can you use sound to create your desired reality?
 - What successful programming will you listen to today?

CHAPTER 8

Speech:

Activating Your Quantum Creation Field

The afternoon sun beeped behind the mountains as I sat across from Elena, as the successful CEO, shared her revelation. "I never realized my words were creating my reality," she said, her voice filled with wonder. "I've been speaking struggle into existence."

Her insight perfectly captures the quantum power of speech in reality creation.

Dr. Masaru Emoto's revolutionary research reveals something extraordinary about spoken words: They create measurable changes in physical reality.

When you speak, you're not just communicating - you're literally sending instructions to the quantum field through what physicists call "coherent vibration patterns."

Consider this: Every word you speak creates an electromagnetic signature that extends several feet beyond your body. Recent studies using quantum field detectors show that positive speech creates coherent energy patterns that attract similar frequencies, while negative speech creates chaotic patterns that repel success.

Let me share Robert's transformation story. As a venture capitalist, he was successful but struggled with consistent growth until he understood the power of conscious speech. His default language patterns included:
- "I'll try to make it happen"

- "It's going to be difficult"
- "I hope it works out"
- "The market is challenging"

Through conscious speech practices, he transformed his language to:
- "I am creating this reality"
- "This is unfolding perfectly"
- "Success is inevitable"
- "Opportunities are abundant"

The transformation was remarkable. Within three months:
- His investment returns doubled
- Team alignment improved dramatically
- Deal flow increased naturally
- Stress levels dropped significantly

Take a moment now. Record yourself speaking about your goals for five minutes. Play it back and notice your speech patterns. Are your words creating or limiting your desired reality?

Recent quantum physics research shows that conscious speech literally alters the electromagnetic field around you, creating what scientists call "reality attraction patterns."

Create your success speech protocol:
1. Identify limiting language patterns
2. Craft empowering replacements
3. Practice conscious speech daily

4. Monitor reality shifts

Practice quantum speech meditation:
1. Sit quietly with eyes closed
2. Feel the power of your voice
3. Speak your desired reality
4. Feel the vibration creating change

Remember: Your speech is either activating success or programming limitation.

The choice isn't whether you're creating through speech - you're doing that with every word.

The choice is what reality you choose to speak into existence.

In Chapter 9, we'll explore how to integrate all four OWLS components for maximum transformation. You're not just learning about speech - you're mastering the art of quantum reality creation through conscious language.

Before moving forward, consider:
 - What reality are your words creating?
 - How can you use speech to accelerate success?
 - What will you speak into existence today?

CHAPTER 9

The Integration:

Mastering the OWLS System

The morning light filtered through the office window as Brian, a technology CEO, shared his breakthrough moment. "I've been using each component of OWLS separately," he said, "but something magical happened when I integrated them."

His experience perfectly captures the quantum power of system integration in conscious reality creation.

Dr. Bruce Lipton's groundbreaking research reveals something extraordinary about integrated practices: When multiple consciousness tools are used together, they create what he calls a "biological amplification effect."

Your brain literally processes integrated practices differently than isolated ones, creating what neuroscientists call "enhanced neural coherence."

Consider this: While each component of OWLS - Observation, Writing, Listening, and Speech - is powerful alone, together they create what quantum physicists call a "reality resonance field." This field literally amplifies your creative power exponentially.

Let me share Victoria's transformation story. As a successful entrepreneur, she had tried various success practices but struggled with consistent results until she understood the power of integration.

Her breakthrough came when she created what we call a "Reality Creation Ritual":

Morning Integration Practice:
 - Conscious observation of emerging opportunities (10 minutes)
 - Success script writing in her transformation journal (15 minutes)
 - Strategic success audio programming during preparation (20 minutes)
 - Powerful declarations of intended outcomes (5 minutes)

The transformation was remarkable. Within two months:
 - Her business revenue tripled
 - Team alignment improved dramatically
 - Innovation became effortless
 - Stress dissolved naturally

Create your integrated practice now:
 1. Find a quiet space
 2. Observe your current reality with awareness
 3. Write your intended reality in present tense
 4. Listen to success programming
 5. Speak your reality into existence

Recent studies using quantum field detectors show that integrated practices create coherent energy patterns up to 100 times stronger than isolated practices.

Design your daily reality creation protocol:
- Morning power hour using all OWLS components
- Midday reality alignment check
- Evening integration and celebration
- Nighttime subconscious programming

Practice integrated consciousness meditation:
1. Sit in your creation space
2. Engage all OWLS components simultaneously
3. Feel the amplified field of possibility
4. Allow transformation to emerge naturally

Remember: Integration isn't about doing more - it's about creating coherence.

The question isn't whether you're using these tools - you're always using them.

The question is: Are you using them in harmony or in chaos?

In Chapter 10, we'll explore how to maintain this integrated practice during challenges. You're not just learning techniques - you're becoming a master of conscious reality creation.

Before moving forward, consider:
- How can you integrate OWLS more fully
- What reality will you create through integration?
- When will you begin your integrated practice?

CHAPTER 10

Mastering Resistance:

When Reality Tests Your Creation

It was an unusually a quiet afternoon as Michael, a seasoned entrepreneur, shared his challenge. "The OWLS system works beautifully when things are flowing," he said, "but what about when reality seems to resist your creation?"

His question perfectly captures the crucial moment in every creator's journey - when your new programming meets established patterns.

Dr. Joe Dispenza's latest research reveals something fascinating about resistance: When you begin changing your reality creation patterns, your brain initially creates what neuroscientists call a "neural protest" - a temporary increase in opposing thoughts and emotions.

This isn't failure - it's evidence of transformation in progress.

Consider this: Every quantum leap in your reality is preceded by a period of apparent resistance. Recent studies at the HeartMath Institute show that when you maintain coherent creation practices during resistance, you actually accelerate your transformation by up to 300%.

Let me share Alexandra's breakthrough story. As a successful corporate executive transitioning to entrepreneurship, she encountered intense resistance when implementing the OWLS system.

Her initial experience included:
- Increased doubt and fear thoughts
- Physical discomfort during practices
- Temporary financial fluctuations
- Relationship challenges

Instead of retreating, she deepened her practice:
- Observed resistance without judgment
- Wrote about challenges as opportunities
- Listened to advanced success programming
- Spoke power into apparent obstacles

The transformation was remarkable. Within four months:
- Her new business surpassed her corporate income
- Relationships transformed positively
- Innovation flowed naturally
- Inner peace became her normal state

Take a moment now. Identify your current biggest resistance point. Close your eyes and feel into it. Notice how resistance isn't opposing your creation - it's actually revealing where transformation is most potent.

Recent brain imaging studies show that maintaining conscious creation practices during resistance literally accelerates neural reorganization, creating what scientists call "breakthrough pathways."

Create your resistance mastery protocol:
1. Document current resistance points

2. Design specific OWLS responses
3. Track breakthrough patterns
4. Celebrate resistance as transformation

Practice resistance transformation meditation:
1. Sit with your biggest challenge
2. Feel it fully without resistance
3. Apply OWLS components consciously
4. Experience transformation emerging

Remember: Resistance isn't opposing your creation - it's revealing where your creative power is most needed.
The question isn't whether you'll encounter resistance - you will.
The question is: Will you use it as fuel for transformation?

In Chapter 11, we'll explore how to expand your creation field beyond personal reality. You're not just learning to handle resistance - you're mastering the art of turning apparent obstacles into breakthrough opportunities.

Before moving forward, consider:
 - How can you use resistance as fuel?
 - What breakthrough is currently emerging?
 - Where will you apply your creative power today?

CHAPTER 11

The Field Effect:
Creating Collective Reality

The brightness of the sun illuminated the office, I squinted as Rachel, a transformational leader, shared her latest insight.
"Something extraordinary happened when I expanded my creation field beyond myself," she said. "My entire organization began transforming."

Her experience perfectly illustrates the quantum principle of field effect in conscious reality creation.

Dr. William Tiller's groundbreaking research at Stanford reveals something remarkable:

Your conscious creation field extends far beyond your personal reality. When you maintain coherent creation practices, you generate what quantum physicists call an "intentional coherence field" that influences collective reality up to 300 feet in every direction.

Consider this: Every thought you think, every word you speak, every reality you create ripples through the quantum field, affecting not just your experience but the collective field of possibility.

Recent studies using quantum field detectors show that one person maintaining coherent creation practices can positively influence up to 100,000 people.
Let me share Daniel's transformation story. As a business leader, he discovered that applying the

OWLS system created ripple effects throughout his organization:

Initial Personal Practice:
- Observing opportunities for collective growth
- Writing visions for team success
- Listening to advanced leadership content
- Speaking empowering truths to his team

The collective transformation was remarkable. Within six months:
- Company revenue increased by 200%
- Team engagement soared
- Innovation became cultural
- Stress levels dropped organization-wide

Take a moment now. Close your eyes and feel your creation field extending beyond your personal space. Notice how your consciousness influences the collective field. This awareness is the first step in conscious collective creation.

Recent studies using advanced electromagnetic sensors show that coherent creation practices create measurable changes in the surrounding quantum field, influencing both people and physical reality.

Expand your creation field:
1. Start with personal coherence
2. Extend to immediate environment
3. Expand to organizational level
4. Influence global consciousness

Practice field expansion meditation:
1. Center in personal coherence
2. Feel your field expanding
3. Connect with collective consciousness
4. Create from unified awareness

Remember: Your creation field isn't limited to personal reality.

The question isn't whether you're influencing collective reality - you're doing that every moment.

The question is: Are you influencing it consciously or unconsciously?

In Chapter 12, we'll explore how to maintain expanded field coherence during global transformation. You're not just creating personal reality - you're participating in collective evolution.

Before moving forward, consider:
- How does your creation field affect others?
- What collective reality will you influence?
- How will you expand your impact today?

CHAPTER 12

Quantum Resilience:
Creating in Times of Change

On a warm summer afternoon, I sat down with Hannah, a global business leader, who shared her concern. "The world is changing so rapidly," she said. "How do we maintain our creation field in such uncertainty?"

Her question perfectly captures the challenge of conscious creation in our transformational times.

Dr. Gregg Braden's latest research reveals something extraordinary about creation during change: When global fields are in flux, individual creation fields can actually become more powerful.

It's similar to how a small coherent signal can influence a larger chaotic system - a principle quantum physicists call "coherent resonance."

Consider this: In times of great change, most people contract into survival patterns, weakening their creation field.

But those who maintain conscious creation practices during uncertainty generate resilient coherence - a state that actually amplifies their creative power.

Let me share Marcus's transformation story. As a technology innovator, he discovered that global uncertainty provided unique opportunities for conscious creation:

His Initial Response to Change:
- Observed emerging possibilities rather than problems
- Wrote expanded visions during market shifts
- Listened to advanced transformation content
- Spoke certainty into uncertain situations

The transformation was remarkable. During six months of market volatility:
- His company's market share tripled
- Team resilience strengthened
- Innovation accelerated
- Stability emerged from chaos

Take a moment now. Close your eyes and feel into current global changes. Notice how uncertainty actually reveals new possibilities. This awareness is the first step in quantum resilience.

Recent studies using quantum field detectors show that coherent creation practices become up to 500% more effective during periods of collective transformation.

Create your resilience protocol:
1. Map current change patterns
2. Identify creation opportunities
3. Maintain OWLS practices daily
4. Track breakthrough moments

Practice quantum resilience meditation:
1. Center in your creation field

2. Feel global transformation waves
3. Maintain coherent creation
4. Experience expanded possibility

Remember: Change isn't opposing your creation - it's providing enhanced creative potential.

The question isn't whether you'll face uncertainty - you will.

The question is: Will you use it to amplify your creative power?

In Chapter 13, we'll explore how to expand your creation field into new dimensions of possibility. You're not just creating through change - you're using transformation as a catalyst for quantum leaps.

Before moving forward, consider:
 -How can you use current changes as creative fuel?
 -What possibilities are emerging through transformation?
 -Where will you direct your enhanced creative power?

CHAPTER 13

The Language of Creation:

Words That Shape Words

I leaned back in my chair as Jennifer, a transformation coach, shared her breakthrough. "When I changed my language patterns," she said, "my entire reality shifted overnight."

Her experience perfectly illustrates what quantum linguistics reveals about the power of conscious speech in reality creation.

Dr. Leonard Laskow's research reveals something extraordinary about language: Your words create specific electromagnetic frequencies that interact directly with the quantum field.

When you speak, you're not just communicating - you're literally programming the field of infinite possibilities.

Consider this: Every word you speak creates a ripple effect in the quantum field that extends for up to 48 hours.

Recent studies using advanced quantum field detectors show that positive, empowered speech creates coherent energy patterns that attract similar frequencies, while limiting language creates interference patterns that block manifestation.

Let me share Alexandra's transformation story. As a successful entrepreneur, she discovered that her language patterns were creating unconscious resistance to her desired reality:

Her Default Language Patterns:
- "I'll try to make it happen"
- "Hopefully it works out"
- "If everything goes well"
- "I'm not sure if I can"

Through conscious language reprogramming, she transformed her speech to:
- "I am creating this now"
- "Success is inevitable"
- "Everything works in my favor"
- "I am fully capable"

The transformation was remarkable. Within three months:
- Her business revenue doubled
- Team alignment strengthened naturally
- Innovation became effortless
- Stress dissolved completely

Take a moment now. Record yourself speaking about your goals for five minutes. Play it back and notice your language patterns. Are your words creating or limiting your desired reality?

Recent studies using quantum field measurement devices show that conscious speech creates coherent energy patterns up to 100 times stronger than unconscious speech.

Create your language mastery protocol:
1. Document current speech patterns

2. Design empowered replacements
3. Practice conscious speech daily
4. Track reality shifts

Practice quantum speech meditation:
1. Center in silence
2. Feel the power of your voice
3. Speak your reality into existence
4. Experience immediate shifts

Remember: Your words aren't just describing your reality - they're creating it.

The question isn't whether your speech is programming the quantum field - it is.

The question is: What reality are you choosing to create through your words?

In Chapter 14, we'll explore how to maintain empowered speech during challenges. You're not just learning about language - you're mastering the art of quantum creation through conscious speech.

CHAPTER 14

The Momentum Principle:

Sustaining Your Creation Field

The late afternoon sun cast golden shadows as Michael, a business innovator, shared his insight. "The real breakthrough came when I stopped treating transformation as an event and started seeing it as a momentum game," he said.

His experience perfectly captures the quantum principle of sustained creation.

Dr. Andrew Huberman's latest research reveals something fascinating about sustained transformation:

When you maintain conscious creation practices for at least 66 days, your brain creates what neuroscientists call "automated success pathways" - neural networks that make transformation your default state rather than your struggle.

Consider this: Every conscious creation practice builds momentum in your quantum field. Recent studies using advanced coherence mapping show that consistent practice creates what researchers call a "success cascade" - where each small win automatically triggers larger transformations.

Let me share Rebecca's transformation story.
As a tech entrepreneur, she discovered that momentum was the key to quantum creation:

Her Initial Approach (Event-Based):
 - Random bursts of inspiration

- Sporadic practice sessions
- Inconsistent results
- Frequent setbacks

Her Momentum Approach:
- Daily conscious creation rituals
- Consistent OWLS practice
- Progressive wins celebration
- Continuous field expansion

The transformation was remarkable. Within four months:
- Her company's growth became exponential
- Team alignment strengthened naturally
- Innovation became automatic
- Success became her default state

Take a moment now. Map your current creation momentum. Notice where you're building speed and where you're creating resistance. This awareness is the first step in momentum mastery.

Recent studies using quantum field measurements show that consistent practice creates cumulative effects, with each day of practice amplifying your creation field by up to 4%.

Create your momentum protocol:
1. Design daily creation rituals
2. Track progressive wins
3. Celebrate small victories
4. Build success momentum

Practice momentum meditation:
1. Center in your creation field
2. Feel your current momentum
3. Amplify success patterns
4. Experience accelerated creation

Remember: Momentum isn't about intensity - it's about consistency.

The question isn't whether you're building momentum - you are.
The question is: Are you building it consciously or randomly?

In Chapter 15, we'll explore how to use momentum for quantum leaps in reality creation. You're not just maintaining practices - you're creating an unstoppable force of transformation.

CHAPTER 15

Quantum Leaps:

Accelerating Your Reality Creation

The cloudy day casted shadows as David, a transformation leader, shared his breakthrough. "I discovered that quantum leaps aren't random," he said. "They happen when momentum meets conscious intention."

His insight perfectly captures the science of accelerated reality creation.

Research reveals something extraordinary about transformation: When you maintain coherent creation practices while building momentum, you create what quantum physicists call "phase transition points" - moments where reality can shift dramatically in an instant.

Consider this: Every quantum leap appears sudden to observers but is actually the result of consistent conscious creation practices.

Recent studies using quantum field mapping show that what looks like overnight success is really the culmination of coherent momentum reaching critical mass.

Let me share Isabella's transformation story. As a conscious entrepreneur, she discovered the secret to quantum leaps:

Her Previous Approach:
 - Pushing for results
 - Forcing transformation

- Resisting current reality
- Doubting the process

Her Quantum Approach:
- Building coherent momentum
- Allowing transformation
- Embracing present reality
- Trusting the process

The transformation was remarkable. Within two months:
- Her impact multiplied tenfold
- Opportunities emerged effortlessly
- Innovation became natural
- Success became inevitable

Take a moment now. Feel into your current momentum field. Notice where you're pushing and where you're allowing. This awareness is the first step in quantum acceleration.

Recent studies using advanced coherence mapping show that quantum leaps occur when your creation field maintains consistent coherence for at least 21 days.

Create your quantum leap protocol:
1. Map your momentum points
2. Identify resistance patterns
3. Maintain coherent practices
4. Allow accelerated transformation

Practice quantum acceleration meditation:
1. Center in your creation field
2. Feel your building momentum
3. Release all resistance
4. Experience quantum acceleration

Remember: Quantum leaps aren't about force - they're about coherence meeting momentum.
The question isn't whether you'll experience quantum leaps - you will.

The question is: Are you allowing them or resisting them?

In Chapter 16, we'll explore how to maintain stability during quantum leaps. You're not just creating change - you're mastering the art of accelerated transformation.

CHAPTER 16

Identity Shift:

Becoming Your Future Self Now

The setting sun painted the sky in amber hues as Emma, a conscious creator, shared her deepest insight. "The real quantum leap happened when I stopped trying to change my reality and started embodying my future self," she said.

Her revelation perfectly captures the essence of identity-based transformation.

Research reveals something extraordinary about identity: When you shift your identity at the quantum level, your brain literally begins operating from your future self's neural patterns. Maxwell Maltz, MD famously illustrates the true worthiness lies in self-image and the way we look at ourselves.

You're not just changing what you do - you're becoming who you need to be to create your desired reality.

Consider this: Every moment you're either reinforcing your current identity or stepping into your future self. Recent studies using advanced brain mapping show that identity shifts create what neuroscientists call "future memory patterns" - neural networks that operate as if your desired future is already your present reality.

Let me share Thomas's transformation story. As a business visionary, he discovered the power of identity shifting:

His Previous Approach:
- Working harder to achieve goals
- Trying to prove his worth
- Struggling with imposter syndrome
- Doubting his capabilities

His Identity Shift Approach:
- Daily embodying his future self
- Operating from innate worth
- Embracing natural leadership
- Knowing his infinite potential

The transformation was remarkable. Within six weeks:
- His leadership impact tripled
- Team performance soared
- Innovation became effortless
- Success became inevitable

Take a moment now. Close your eyes and step into your future self's consciousness. Feel how they think, move, and create. This isn't visualization - it's identity activation.
Recent studies using quantum field measurements show that identity shifts create coherent energy patterns up to 1000 times stronger than behavioral changes alone.

Create your identity shift protocol:
1. Map your future self's traits
2. Embody their consciousness daily

3. Operate from their reality
4. Allow natural transformation

Practice identity shift meditation:
1. Center in present awareness
2. Connect with your future self
3. Merge consciousnesses
4. Operate from expanded identity

Remember: Identity isn't fixed - it's a choice you make at every moment.
The question isn't whether you're creating an identity - you are.

The question is: Are you consciously choosing who you're becoming?

In Chapter 17, we'll explore how to maintain your expanded identity during daily challenges. You're not just changing your reality - you're becoming the conscious creator you were meant to be.

CHAPTER 17

Field Mastery:

Advanced Reality Creation

I stare across the desk as Ethan, a master creator, shared his deepest insight. "The quantum field isn't just responding to our intentions," he said, "it's responding to our state of being."

His observation perfectly captures the essence of advanced reality creation.

Dr. William Tiller's groundbreaking research reveals something extraordinary about consciousness: When you achieve what quantum physicists call "coherent being states," your reality creation power increases by up to 5000%.

You're not just thinking about your desired reality - you're emanating it from your very being.

Consider this: Every moment, your consciousness is either in a state of coherent creation or unconscious reaction. Recent studies using quantum field sensors show that coherent being states create what researchers call "reality attraction vortexes" - fields of possibility that naturally draw your desired reality into physical manifestation.

Let me share Victoria's transformation story. As a consciousness pioneer, she discovered the power of being states:

Her Previous Approach:
 - Focusing on doing more
 - Trying to control outcomes

- Pushing against resistance
- Struggling with uncertainty

Her Being State Approach:
- Emanating success consciousness
- Allowing natural unfolding
- Embracing all experiences
- Dancing with uncertainty

The transformation was remarkable. Within eight weeks:
- Her impact became exponential
- Synchronicities multiplied
- Creation became effortless
- Reality began serving her vision

Take a moment now. Close your eyes and shift from doing to being. Feel the difference between trying to create and allowing creation through you. This is field mastery in action.

Recent studies using advanced coherence mapping show that states create reality shifts up to 100 times faster than action-based approaches.

Create your field mastery protocol:
1. Map your current being state
2. Design your desired state
3. Practice state shifting
4. Allow natural manifestation

Practice being state meditation:
1. Release all doing
2. Enter pure being
3. Feel your creation field
4. Allow reality to align

Remember: Your being state is your most powerful creation tool.

The question isn't whether you're creating from a being state - you are.

The question is: What reality is your current state emanating?

Let's explore how to maintain these advanced states during daily life. You're not just creating reality - you're becoming a master of consciousness itself.

CHAPTER 18

The Awakening:
Your Journey Begins Now

The afternoon breeze drifted in through the window as Jennifer, a master creator, shared her final insight. "The most powerful moment," she said, "was realizing that mastery isn't a destination - it's an eternal dance with infinite possibility."

Her words perfectly capture the essence of conscious creation.

Consider this profound truth: Everything you've learned in this journey - from the OWLS system to quantum field mastery - comes down to one fundamental reality.

You are not just experiencing reality - you are the conscious creator of it. Every thought, every word, every state of being is either expanding or limiting your creation field.

Let me share Clara's integration story. As a consciousness pioneer, she discovered how to weave all elements into a unified creation practice:

Her Quantum Integration:
 - Observation became natural awareness
 - Writing transformed into reality programming
 - Listening evolved to quantum attunement
 - Speech became reality activation
 - Being states emerged effortlessly
 - Creation became automatic

The transformation was remarkable. Within three months:
- Her impact became exponential
- Reality began serving her vision
- Innovation flowed naturally
- Success became inevitable

But here's what makes this moment powerful: You're not just holding a book of knowledge - you're holding a blueprint for consciousness transformation. Every principle, every practice, every insight is designed to awaken your innate creator.

Take a moment now. Feel into your expanded creation field. Notice how different you are from when you began this journey. This isn't just change - it's evolution.

Recent studies show that integrated consciousness practices create what quantum physicists call a "reality mastery field" - a state where creation becomes your natural way of being.

Create your mastery protocol:
1. Maintain daily OWLS practices
2. Embody your future self
3. Allow quantum acceleration
4. Trust the process completely

Practice creator consciousness meditation:
1. Center in your mastery
2. Feel your infinite potential

3. Embrace your creator nature
4. Begin your eternal dance

Remember: This isn't the end of your journey - it's the beginning of your conscious creation adventure.

The question isn't whether you'll create your reality - you will.
The question is: What reality will you choose to create?

Before closing this book, consider:
 - Who have you become through this journey?
 - What reality are you ready to create?
 - How will you use your creator power?

Your journey of conscious creation begins now.

Not tomorrow, not when conditions are perfect, but in this moment of awareness. You have everything you need to transform your reality.

The only question is: Are you ready to become the conscious creator you were born to be?

The power is yours.
The time is now.
Your conscious creation journey begins.

Key takeaways from the Quantum Mindset

O -Observe: become the active observer. Observed the life experiences you wish to experience while de-escalating the emotional attachment you have to the experiences you don't wish to experience.

W -Writing: journaling is the key to success but only if you're writing positive affirmations and goal oriented tasks to move you along the right path. Refrain from writing about trauma instead, consciously write the experiences you want to experience.

L -Listening: be aware of what you are listening to. Remember everything is programming you whether you're aware of it or not. Music, movies and the people you communicate with on a regular basis are all influencing your mind. Become the gatekeeper of your mind don't allow toxic information in.

S -Speech: every word you speak carries a frequency. Speak good over your life and over the lives of others to see your reality shift and change. Stay away from gossip or negative talk about yourself or about others.

Thank you for taking time to learn about the OWLS system. With consistency I know this will bless your life and transform you into the greatest version of yourself.

ABOUT THE AUTHOR

Alia Yasmin Khan is a distinguished thought leader, international best-selling author, and speaker with over two decades of experience in business management and mindset coaching.

She is the founder of "Sublime Knowledge", a mindset coaching company based in Phoenix, Arizona, which she established in 2022.

Alia's journey to becoming a mindset coach was shaped by her personal struggles with emotional distress

Through her own transformation, she developed a profound understanding of the mind's inner workings and now helps others achieve their goals in areas such as love, wealth, and health.

Her, coaching philosophy emphasizes aligning thoughts, feelings, and belief with personal goals to create positive change.

Alia is also a co-author of the international bestseller "Succeeding in Business in Any Market, Vol. 2" and is passionate about empowering individuals to master their minds and live fulfilling lives.

www.ingramcontent.com/pod-product-compliance
Lightning Source LLC
Chambersburg PA
CBHW020551030426
42337CB00013B/1042